KADDY

The Ti

SALT

CROMER

PUBLISHED BY SALT PUBLISHING 2018

2 4 6 8 10 9 7 5 3 1

First published in Great Britain in 2018 by
Salt Publishing Ltd
12 Norwich Road, Cromer, Norfolk NR27 0AX United Kingdom

www.saltpublishing.com

Salt Publishing Limited Reg. No. 5293401

A CIP catalogue record for this book is available from the British Library

ISBN 978 1 78463 158 1 (Paperback edition)

Typeset in Sabon by Salt Publishing

Printed and bound in Great Britain by Clays Ltd, Elcograf S.p.A.

for Mary

Stiùir thu gu Eilean Eige mi;
stiùir thu mi air falbh bhon eilean a th' annam fhìn

Contents

BONE HOUSES: SKYE

Seven Letters Home: Touchstone

Balanced on the map of my palm
there's a sense of a different ending;
each threaded vein of it
reaches beyond the pebble's edge
and connects to the carved pink leys
and channels of my skin. Here –
a heart line not stopping at loss

breaks free to ramble now
in search of finer trails: scents, spores,
traces of life unsevered by my other hand.
There – a new passage overlays
a violet twist of hate and shame, wipes
out a fatal double-helix long enough
to let this gift's bright tributaries

reroute the past and navigate
a continent of trust. My heart's needle
shivers, spins, settling for a true
north where this wanderlust
must begin, must end; each new
territory crossed taking me further
from her touchstone, closer to myself.

Megalosaurus

Those moments when you close ears,
eyes, to take in a dinosaur site
then a child interrupts, limb-twisting,
and urgently needing a piss
so you shield her with a wind-cracking anorak
while she squats over a cattle-grid –

and misses –
kicks up a fuss at the steaming splash-back
litmussing her jeans, suckers off,
welly-prints sunk in antediluvian mud.

Those moments
when you almost don't notice
the way a river runnels around islets
of dry shingle, the stilled mill behind you
with its atmosphere of collapse,
a long-dead ewe laid out on a boulder:

bleached to the bone, ringlets of wet fleece
shrink-wrapped over Jurassic stone
as though fallen through history
having jettisoned flesh just to get there.

Bone Houses

Settlers long-dead, their chattels gulped
deep inside the mire with every saline tide.
They rise, awaken that fear in me: being held

for centuries, my bonetight leathers
preserved and warped in layered darkness.
I stumble across reed sumps and sand piles

where shy birds hide and flies seek dun,
low-bellied cows hard at their indolent munching.
I stagger the sunken coast road, its salt-crusted

brinks, its mounds of broken harvests,
smatterings of shattered scapulae. I lurch
into a ditch, let a milk-haired farmer speed by

hauling a trailer of mulched peat at the back of
a clapped-out silver Maestro. I spy inside.
On the blanketed back seat: a metal detector,

samphire, the blue carcass of a salt marsh lamb.
Imagine him bent at a kitchen table, sifting
his darkened haul through cracked black fingers,

culling out the bones of a new work – the unfastened
bones, black bones, dried and unfastened –
licking his lips as the lamb fat crackles, spits.

Seven Letters Home: Ammonite

Somewhere outside the bone
museum the air splinters and bleeds.

I split a nail digging for waterproofs,
let my young stamp ire into liquid mirrors

as I test my pocket for flickers of life.
Now where? they howl. *Nowhere,*

I murmur, scrolling old voicemails
for the one that makes my smile unfurl

like an ammonite freed from its tight stone
bed; the one that lets me treasure

her fossil voice wishing I was elsewhere
or anywhere, anywhere but here.

Mearl

My daughter tells me her body
has 270 bones, reducing
to 206 between child and adulthood.

I'm musing on this as we leap streams,
run palms along the powdered
spines of falling walls and try not

to cry at a cow's infected eyes.
We're heading for the coral
beach: Skye's slice of the Caribbean,

where a cove of calcified seaweed
bits shines white as a bone-
yard, bright as a cup of bleached beads.

We sift the pale gravel, scoop handfuls
into a wrinkled paper bag:
hundreds of unsugared thousands.

Observing our dusted hands sink
and lift and sink again
inside this disintegrating grit, I miss

the fused bones of my godmother's
arthritic fingers: puffed knuckles,
wilted skin; the bliss of unhurried touch.

A Sudden Fall of Water

Ten days after she dies
I'm hiking the Black
Cuillin in a freakish heat,
the weight of it pushing in on my skin,
my lungs, my dry and puffy eyes.

I am worrying about fluids:
this half-done dinted canteen,
sweat blotches at bloom on my back
an urgent wish to dive inside
the next ice blue corrie or loch
for just the promise of a drop
of it to mollify the loss.

But where has all the water gone?
I see rock-spill drifting the split ravines,
tracks dried up, cracked to nothing
but a flurry. I see burns un-
tumbling, all water fallen silent.

I am itchy with grief,
my grimy cheeks snicked with it
until a rip and snag of my ankle bone
on a crag has me grasp at a collapse;
lets hard rock give way
to a spectacular spill
cascading my crumpled face.

Seven Letters Home: Succulent

Driving in a north easterly, the crimped
tumid sprig cradled in a compostable mushroom tray

on my lap, my husband distant beside me.
I watch him catch the black winging in the corn,

wonder if he's also thinking *van Gogh*, recall
as a teenager always wanting to fuck

under a heavy swelling of thunderheads.
I place her fleshy cutting on the windowsill

of our room, tick beside it –
back and forth in the rocking chair –

observing its tiny diurnal changes for an inkling
of a root hooking into my Fen-dark soil.

Day by day, something in its dipped swing shape
is a safety net twice over: a memory of the low, low

to-and-fro of her voice, and the rainbow hammock
I read in, daydream in, miss her in as my skin

turns freckled brown and this stem, this stem
she gave me, has time for its do-or-die indecision.

Pulp

From the back
bashes through
her knees thwack
against my seat,
her eye & grin in the wing
my little finger the way
found entrancing.
she either rolls her eyes
naps while I on-and-off watch,
famished, clamouring for the last
She breaks a tooth on it
& lakes hemming the edges
yelps & lunges forward
the socket, then drops
in the sweet tin
I examine it: little petal,
pale as chalk &
At dusk, stretching
in this heather-dense
for her hot florid cheeks
dribble & grizzle;
against my lips.
this as I rest at a split fir
lightning-struck & singed
centre shocked apart
raw & naked,

a thrash of bass
her headphones,
infrequently
she scowls if I catch
mirror, wriggle
her baby self
These days
or blanks me,
wakes ratty &
barley twist.
as we skirt fells
of the highlands;
for a tissue to mop
the bloodied chip
for safekeeping.
opal, its marrow
fragile to the core.
my aching limbs
landscape, I'll long
again; how she would
those forearm creases
I'll remember all
uprooted above the croft,
to a tinder, its tender
from the blackened bark,
the pulp of its heart.

Poor Tree

after Poor Tom *by Tom de Freston & Simon Palfrey*

Far off, a band of firs
marches down a mountainside
slipped with shale and gritstone.
But she wants this one,
and this one alone in its patch
of scrub: this stunted birch.

She visits it in the night-time
strips herself deliberately beneath
its forked animal branches,
naked to naked, deranged and faithful,
her hair in snarls, her face
mired in clay until disguised

and eye-blind: filthy. Out here
on the heath, she honours her disorder,
enacts chaos by living out a thing
beneath human level, the fractures
of herself shivering a gibberish,
alive or dead – *is cold, is cold.*

A storm of midges billows for her skin
bringing in a darkness like cliff-
edge, or the threat of it.
Teetering at the temptation to leap
from only-just-holding-on she bellows:
Really, must I beg for it? Must I?

Seven Letters Home: Pipistrelle

Kitchen sleepless 2am,
a car approaches on the lane,

headlights sweeping the room
like a night watchman

so I hide. Hide
beside the windowsill

stroking the stiff black pouch
of a skate's embryo sac –

dried pipistrelle from the sea.
I think about the night we swam

beneath milk-lipped waves:
how we rose, we fell,

caught in the suck and swell
of a sleeping creature's breathing.

Little Minch

As if a Lilliput name could
diminish this vicious stretch
filled brimful of basking
shark, sea litter & storm
kelpies. Some call it the
stream of the blue men:
their long grey faces &
salt-glazed eyes strobing
convulsively for sea dogs
lost long enough to lug into
the pit of an ice-black sea.
Little Minch – capricious
bitch – how you hound me
and lap at my heels; love me
unpredictably, nuzzle at my
pulse, before tugging me
under & under & under.
You despise it if I tug my
eyes from you yet chide me
if I come too close to find-
ing a safe passage between
the I-lands of my selves.

My Water Bull

To swim with my husband
    is to witness a panicking animal
        that shouldn't be let near water.
I am reminded of this watching him
    cling to the side of the swimming
        pool as our younglings thrash

and dive and leap about
    like a pair of goggle-eyed smolts.
        His expression is one of fear:
fear that calves its own new fear
    into me; fear I must wade away from.
        This morning, before a rain-haze

forced us into retreat, we followed
    the old drove road to Staffin Bay.
        And while the kids bickered
in the back and my husband listed
    to get a signal, I spied the remains
        of a fishing station just across

the water, its poles once used
    to dry nets, but now repurposed
        for a shieling. There was once
a farmer lived there who loved
    with his whole heart a fat herd
        of shaggy black-coated cattle

raised to trade with the lowlands
     for barley, honey, oats. At neap tides,
         knowing that the lush island grass
was better for grazing, he'd swim
    his cows gently across the loch, each
         beast tied to the tail of the one in front.

Seven Letters Home: Crow

I imagine telling her about my lazy day
in the hammock slung between two silvers,
my children haring about in wild garlic,
hollering, rubbing mud on their palms,
their bellies; making potions from sprig-
ripped lavender, windfalls, dew, and rose
petals on the turn. I want to show her my son:
his first loose tooth swinging like a cat-
flap as he pokes at a dead fox with a stick,
upends an unholy stench of rancid flesh;
his fearful curiosity as I explain (again
and again) the cycle of rot and return,
how only life then its absence can do that.
I want to describe my distant daughter:
the way she splays her raised hands, pivots
on one foot and spins through a cartwheel
like a pheasant shot from the sky, or the crow,
guardian of the gate post: its fanned tail, a crack
of wings, the draft as it lands in the branch
overhead, flinging its shadow across me, briefly.

Skye, Diving

i.m. Carol Dykstra

I'm wading through heather,
razor grass, tripping
over mounds and stepping-stones

toward the hope of a waterfall,
deep green cols. I stop
to snap the imposing purple

of a mountain spur, slip
hurriedly down a skinny, scree-
littered path then sit to see it:

her stepped river.
How long do I watch it emptying
pocket after pocketful

of glacial waste into hasty water?
How soon before it gives me
the urge to undress?

I stand, toes curled over rock-
edge then tip forward
and gently, gently – I fly –

inside spindrifts
and downdraughts of warm air
until I break the river's

skin and an open-mouthed shock
swallows me.
Like skirt, I kick it free,

swim deeper beneath weeds
and crag-arches to find
just the right river-glyphed stone:

one that retains the snow
it was borne from; cools this grieving
fever; works perfectly on her grave.

Into the Wreck
after Adrienne Rich

Child, sleek beneath the pool's skin,
    presses her belly to its bed, listens
to the nearby faraway unwilling,
        yet, to resurface to the force &
    gloam of synchronised smiles.
She lugs her cargo of oxygen ever
        lower, scratches *I Am* into the debris
    & silt to ensure some message of herself
endures there untroubled, untroubling.

        Once upon a time, you were that child
    too: no story or myth you could cling to,
unable to move in your new element,
        you dredged unnavigable depths,
    mining them for so much more
than the tight hold of primal waters;
        your blank eyes perpetually rolling
    toward the single entry/exit point –
a portal minus directions

        on where to capture what was lost.
    You were that bloated, unsmiling child,
blind child watching her father carve
        woman from stone or whittled rib.
    Mother: haunted figurehead who sank
full-breasted nowhere close to your
        gaping mouth, never managing to latch
    on to the need to merge love with infant
hunger. Dream of a line secured; dream

of a line tethered to safety in some
body-hot place where you can trust
the rusted compass, wheezing & whirring
in its efforts to spin. Dream of floating
inside the circled arms of a trusted other;
one schooled in every rope signal – she,
who could haul you from that mass
of forest kelp snagging at your ankles;
stalactites sharpening for your smile.

Seven Letters Home: Little One

You're coming home to a stone:
a child petrified she'll not feel
your heat, your song, the scent
of your hair first thing.

You must tell her she was missed
with your fingers: hold her
injured smile, pinch nose, nudge
chin, count every crease and toe

until certain you are both complete.
If she cries, hits out or whimpers,
hold the shaking bird of her
close to your chest, stroke each

downy bone, uncurl her frozen
wings, warm them with your breath
then clasp them tight behind
your neck and whisper *Little One*.

Ramshackle (I)

"It's our right as a sovereign nation to choose immigrants that we think are the likeliest to thrive and flourish and love us."
DONALD TRUMP (Immigration Policy Speech, Phoenix – 31.08.16)

Beyond the loch's slipway, a farm-
    house once whitewashed, now putty
grey, the ruins of mizzle and windrush:

roof punched through, windows kicked
    in, stripped of paint and left to sprawl
in a fank of brambles. A place like this

lets you know you've always lived
    with doors on hinges, floors unbuckled,
roof beams not crashing in.

A low stone wall still holds something in,
    but not much longer, a stack of peat
creels teetering beside a collapsed barn

where a spiral-horned ram has clambered
    to a scrap of rafter, risen up on hind legs
to look out over his kingdom and behoove

a desire for destruction. I crick my neck
    to look up at him, wince away
from his glint-coat, mock gold in refracted light.

~

She once described my mind as *ramshackle*
        and when I take in this site in a powdery
rain there is a slow, slow 'Oh!' moment

where inside and outside collide.
        It's not the mossy, dripping plasterboard,
the cracked lintels, smashed dresser or

upturned mustard armchair rip-seamed
        and spilling its fleece. It's not the sooty
footprints in the chimney rubble, newly

spewed from the hearth or the old scorch
        of long-cooled fires, the flock wallpaper
blistering, the tongue and groove rucking

or the mildewed prints slipping from frames
        and yanking out hangings from walls. It's
the sight of a woman's faded housecoat

hanging tattered on the back of the kitchen
        door that has me stop and utter:
Don't tell me what happened here. Don't tell me.

∼

I run to call the children in from their wool-
        gathering, to tell them on folded knees
about famine years: hard, bitten winters,

sparse fishing, poor or failing crops, greedy
        lairds evicting their half-starved tenants
for being a diseased or damaged populace.

They listen to me glancing at one another
        uneasily, as though I'm as unstable
as the barn; unwavering as the ram.

My whole lifetime spent guessing I am better
        off for not having been displaced or cleared
to make space for a grazing; yet all my life

so little considering the ram and his arrogance.
        Here, I feel strangely dispossessed
from a belief that all is heritable

when beyond objects, all I really own is this:
        an urge to live and witness more fully,
to visit and fix the sites of my dereliction.

Ramshackle (II)

The rusted Dutch barn
on buckling knees

recalls a dream
version of my mother

chapped and hard
at it with a pitchfork:

hair wuthering, cheeks
ruddy, jean-hems

drenched over claggy
boots. Her eyes

(such frantic eyes)
overrun with loss, with

rage, with something
I was too afraid

to recognise but
understood,

somehow, that only
a ruthless displacing

of the hay could
ever hope to eradicate.

Seven Letters Home: Words

made flesh   I'm home
but I cannot feel you
yet   buried in return are seeds
of loss   hurt   the deficits
touch would tell
how I wept on the bathroom floor
held the stone   to fevered eyes
picturing cool-ringed
fingers   on my lids
how I slept numb
and woke
limb-frozen
sweating   wanting nothing
but the rock
of your body   yet
some far off wisdom
insists on letting me know
how my pulse replies
to fingertips
teasing my hair   the bones
of your wrist against my cheek
the rosemary-scented
dip between
shoulder   and lip
where I rest
my head and make up
a new language
from body parts   of speech

ISLAND OF THE BIG WOMEN: EIGG

Volcanic (I)

An Sgùrr,
born from an eruption
of Rùm's fevered
pitchstone, flowing
hot & molten
across the Atlantic's
seabed valleys
to surface
hissing & cooling,
clambering self
over blackened self
to form a stack of layers,
a columnar stump,
an isolated mountain
standing proud
& sheer on three sides.

At
Sweeney's Bothy

I am Sweeney, the whinger,
the scuttler in the valley.
SEAMUS HEANEY

Come here when you're broken and take refuge in this
plywood space with its window wall framing a view
of Rùm in triptych. Kneel before the wicker hamper
on the floor stuffed with sooty gloves, firelighters, the
torn up box of a long-gone year of whisky. Feed the
ravenous fire and learn to cherish the splutter of the
plump orange kettle on its stove-top. Nap in the nook,
the book-lined nook as modern-day cist or cairn or
cave. Work at the desk, antique binoculars at elbow,
lamp bent away from the page and the gentle scent of
lavender sprigs in a hand-thrown vase. Evenings, your
face to the sinking sun, sit on the bench hammered
together from abandoned sleepers and at night take
flight to the mattress in the rafters, a stripped young
birch as railing to keep you in – or to keep what's trou-
blesome out. Let it hold you, curled safe as Sweeney up
his tree. Eye the island in all its darkness as it reduces
to nothing but this black cube: the wind, the hail, the
crackle of the fire dying, your occasional sighs like
ashes settling into themselves. Take in all this and be no
closer to knowing if it's a lunacy that drew you to this
place or if you wandered here to set your madness free.

Birdman of Beinn Bhuidhe
after Trevor Leat

Up there, among half-lit, half-
mapped crags, you might catch him
ankle-trapped between two
rocks. And if you don't catch him,
you might catch sight of him –

his fleeting back, its pelt
of willowy rods twisted inward,
packed downward into spindles of ribs
seasoned from green to rust
long before a downy bud could erupt.

He squats on the edge of movement,
eyes high over moor, pit and cliff,
one withy arm outstretched
as if to lob a shot or call down
his gods from their beak-battered
shells. Days when there is no sighting
him, you might catch the sense
of a bird or a mind in flight;
a mind unsoothed by silence;
a mind rattled by its own animal

sounds: weeping, breathing, eating;
the rush of flames in the grate;
a demented bellowing wind.

Like Sweeney, I have wandered
these seven years, flitting
from island to island-state, uncloaked,
naked, protected by precious little
but this patchy birdwork mask –
its single unpluckable feather fletched
to the back of my draggled head.

Half-life of the Cockle

for Vicky Williamson

They say if you find a whole one,
look at it sideways to see a fulsome, healthy

heart. Surely that's what I've got here,
not-quite-burrowed in the whistling

black sands of Laig Bay, a huge cockle shell
snagged on Rùm's other mountain-tops

and reflected in the shore's damp canvas.
I poke it with my toe, hope for a jumping,

leaping, bivalve; its one muscled digger foot
dragging it back to the Atlantic. I wait –

flip it with my finger but find it meatless,
empty, nothing tender left to protect.

Lifted, its channelled curve fills my palm:
chalky, pale, a silt of dried-up brackish

inlet water. I will it to live, display itself
like a pair of fibrillating wings – but no.

Somewhere in the flotsam of a teal-green sea,
this cast-away has a double, blenched

of all colour, gasping for its other, every bit
as unhinged. Single-winged butterfly; shucked,

discarded husk, did the dragtides never warn
you when it's safe to open, when to shut?

Winifred

after 'Gate to the Isles' & 'Candle, Eigg',
1980 by Winifred Nicholson

Each time I think of her (and I think of her
often) she is sitting in her mackintosh on a stool
before the open door of a tumbledown croft
hunkered beside the Atlantic. She is painting
a forget-me-not gate, swung half open
on a wee Hebridean garden: flowers, clouds, sea –
all movement – yet contained, somehow,
by her ushered-in lilac mountains. She squints
at both the far things and near, a brush-end
in her teeth, whiskery splinters on her lips
as she mixes her own colours with the tips
of weather-bit fingers; traces of soot, chalk
and pigment in her nails, the creases of her palms,

those trails I'd like to follow. She frowns, furrows,
sploshes away from her paint-wet landscape
not stopping at the island's boggy pastures
or fertile hollows, but hiking toward the sgùrr,
leaning wild-haired into the whip of the wind,
plucking blackcurrants by the wayside,
pinching milkwort flowers from their stalks.
Above the pitchstone cliffs, she pulls a prism
from her pocket to consult it for what it knows,
what she knows already, what Goethe knew
too about the life between colours unseen,
unknown. She nods and smiles that kindling smile
from the other side of words which insists:

let the light find you; let the light lose you again,
there is colour in all dark. Later, warmed,
away from caves and the abandoned canvas,
she kneels like a supplicant before a candle
on a whitewashed upon whitewashed sill.
I can almost smell the just-lit match, hear it suck
at the wick and hiss, I can sense the draught,
the flicker. The paint sparks on her smock
recall your midnight Fair Isle jumper, the glossy
pebbles beside your books, the print of a candle
at a window above your desk – how its flame
stays in the mind's eye a lifetime after guttering;
how each time I think of her, I think of you.

On Not Making it to Gamekeeper's Cottage

it seemed at first glance as if an experience so intimate and vital must be kept remote and safe from the cold white light of consciousness which might destroy its glories.

MARION MILNER, *On Not Being Able to Paint*

I was seven when she mixed it:
the indelible blue
of a gate left swung open
long after a mother had bolted.

A mother like me struggling
not to leave, but stay
stapled around her children:
a canvas stretched to its frame.

I wanted to find the cottage
to study where she'd painted it:
the gate that inhabits a liminal space
between restraint and release,

intimacy and distance,
boundaries she'd broken down.
She came here to find the light
she needed to work with

to paint harebells, herb burnet,
blackbirds' feathers arranged in a jar
to catch the day's colours
happening just as they should.

Island of the Big Women

*Eilean nam Ban Mora – the Island of the Big Women
– lived up to its name.*
   CAMILLE DRESSLER, *Eigg: The Story of an Island*

I. COBWEB JENNY

I see her just ahead of me
      in the ferry's underbelly
            as it waits to dock and spill

its cargo of vehicles, food,
      humans. I can tell she is
            given to living this: kitted

out in waterproof slacks,
      a fleece-lined hat, a sturdy
            rucksack in which I spy

dyed yarns, a few spindles,
      two knitting needles tucked
            into its bottle pocket. Later

in the week, I'll notice her
      collie rise up on hind legs,
            nuzzle a slub on her sleeve.

Watching her stroke him, rub
      his velvet ears, makes my skull
            ache for your fingerpads in my hair.

II. ARTICHOKES
for Lucy Conway

On her piano-top
a portrait of a daughter,
and a family of three

globe artichokes
in a flecked pottery bowl,
their dried out pods

rattle-brittle –
purpled, the thistle heads
soft and vibrant, still

pulsing with a rhythmic
charge sprung up
in the botanical blood.

III. MOUNTAIN DEW

A nineteenth century crofter
diverted an underground burn
to a green-lipped cave
in the cliffs below his home.

In it he hid barley, peat
and a blackened pot smuggled
from Inverness. Tipped off
that the highland exciseman

had a mind to come and visit,
he rolled his cask under the blackhouse
bed where his wife – brimful of milk –
lay nursing their two-day bairn.

iv. Queen Moidart's Revenge

Leaving in the blue-
black dark, my torch-lit
track is watery,

diluted;
such an urge to hurtle
the squall, the fear,

to ditch those ghosts
of my Pictish sisters,
who, sent by their queen

to rid her isle
of its Christian incomers,
waited (as requested)

for the monks to finish mass,
before beheading them
one by one.

v. Vulnerable Side Up

I'm trying to fry two eggs
on the gunwale of a glinting boat
rowed widdershins by Maggie.
She's grilling me about what I could bring
to the island – me, whose only bigness
is physical; me who slowly knows
as we come full circle that I have nothing
to offer this place but my soft eggs,

vulnerable side up and flimsy.
I slip them onto a slice of sourdough
pulled already toasted from my breast
pocket and she looks at me sagely,
then nods, takes them in one hand,
tucking the oars behind her with the other.
She tips them to her lips like shucked
oysters, eyes me unbrokenly, swallows.

Nest, Eigg

It was John-the-Bird who warned me
to be careful when out walking the moors
not to step on a hen harrier's nest
camouflaged in the wild gold grass.
I tread warily even inside the bothy,
afraid I may break something,
afraid I may break myself.
I've come to feel sheltered here:
a chick tucked up in its shell-domed sac
and warmed under a yolk of lamplight.
Afternoons, I curl under a tartan blanket:
two oatcakes, a hot tin mug of fennel tea,
leafing through Camille's *History*
of the Island as the light outside putters out.

Night Tidings
after 'Snow in Summer', 2017 by Miranda Boulton

Nightdrift, night shifts it, lifts the lost
        underpainting from a porthole visibility
                in some blue-black depth to the moment

the image rose in you, flowed from feeling
        to thought to brushstroke, as you peered
                in close in a crepuscular hush to discover

this hard-won shade – not quite blue,
        blue-green, petroleum or aquamarine –
                but fringed, somehow, with a tone of

phosphorescence that rises on the night
        tide to emit its firefly glow that, once
                captured in paint, slowly fades through

silver, to grey, to a dappled ash scattered
        on the backs of sea horses and their foals
                galloping through a froth of blossom.

They shake their manes, sprinkling
        the dunes with flecks of lit pollen blazing
                yellow: yellow to hold onto in the lumen

of a spinning wave; yellow of illicit blooms;
        yellow at the heart of all drowned flowers
                lost at high tide, low tide, ebb tide, flood.

Night Shower

After three matted, grimy days I cave,
stoke the fire – log upon log,
hour upon hour – until the bothy

becomes sweatlodge and each filthy
bit of me sticks to my reeking
clothes. Outside it is black, it is howling.

I peel myself to nothing but a headlamp,
her orange bracelet. Door open,
I am scared. Not of mad or axe-men,

but my own unwitnessed whiteness.
Exposed in this wildered, billowing place,
squally suds and hail on my rump,

I jig and gasp, snigger at the wobble
of these barely shared breasts;
the ice-steam rising from my skin.

Roses

after 'Mary', 2016 by Miranda Boulton

Desire: as though flesh
and bone could ever grow

here once more.
A wastepaper basket

brimful of discarded drafts:
fuel for the long night's

fire – fuel
for a burgeoning.

Later, trying to describe
what imprints itself

on my mind overnight
I glance at pages

opening in the flames,
see briefly again, the roses.

Volcanic (II)

Silverblack beads of rain
smurring the window,
a jam jar of orangey water on the sill,
the storm keeping me bothy-bound

and your voice no longer available.
I was taken by it yesterday:
the colour of the heavy-set kettle
on the stove, how it shook furiously –

all rattle and spit – ever
on the cusp of blowing its lid.
Today the fire hardly
sputters to life and I shiver in smoky

fingerless gloves, bite the skin
on my blue-rimmed lips as I paint you
a replica of the silenced kettle
as though this little thing

winging its way back to you
in a sugar-paper envelope could stifle
all the wild in me; snuff
my desire, my violence, my rage.

Storm Gertrude

~

Setting out for the harbour shop
for a stock of matches, tampons, tea

I notice sheep gathering
to a huddle in a field corner,

glance up at the unreadable sky
as if it were sheet music and I blind

but required somehow to follow.
A blaze of sun hits the post-rain lane,

and, dear god, I am bent on reaching you,
restless as a bird on a pylon

as the weather gathers then shifts
and I wait for reconnection,

my pulse pounding from feet to ears:
pick up, pick up, please pick up.

~

Five hundred miles due south
and your voice falters
up the broken line, telling me, I think,

to prepare. You always see them coming;
predict when they'll hit –
a mother's eye fixed on her febrile

child. I lose connection if I move, hold
still, disregard the clouds rotting in the sky;
a sheet of rain steeping my jeans.

I push the phone closer to my ear,
think I hear your chair creak
as you lean in to examine a slow-moving

vortex of white across your screen.
I picture the forecast as wedding photograph:
a tidal bride swept around dance floor

whom you know, can feel it in your bones,
will transmute to a fury one day
that obliterates her husband, her kids.

~

something's in flux   and rising

a white-out silence renders
lamps and radio defunct

lightning strikes night ultraviolet

the island is backlit to bluebell
detonations so fierce I stagger
up ladder to mattress
curl myself into the child
bite down hard on the clung-to rail

a sound gap opens

and fuses me with fear
fear of the finger of god
rock formation ominous above
the waterfall fear
of the bothy as punched lung
sucking in on its own windows
fear of that static thrum
inside my frazzled head

of my sanctum come undone
and gyrated into the sea

The Right to Roam

*Part 1 of the Land Reform (Scotland) Act 2003 gives everyone
statutory access rights to most land and inland water.*

Feeling slightly fathered
beside Eddie in his truck as he drives
me to the pier for a storm-delayed
ferry home. We slow for ewes
and he inhales, smiles,
double-taps his heart with two fingers:

This land is mine, he says, *and hers
and hers . . . and yours too,
you little incomer.* He winks at me, wipes
the steamed-up windscreen with his woolly hat,
lifts the arm-rest and slings
me a KitKat I cannot eat.

Through a forest of moss furring up
the broken window seal,
I glance back at the island I am leaving
untouched; all the places I haven't wandered:
under a washing line, over a garden
fence, through a woodpile,

towards the waterfall calling me
all week. I cannot say why
I ignored them, chastely turned away,
denied myself permission to visit
a common wilderness instead of staying safe –
but nurturing a wish to live it differently.

Mister Bluebell
for Eddie Scott

The land rover passing through mists
disappears into ghost weather as I wave

to his watery eyes in the vanishing
rearview mirror. A week home, a note

arrives, and I feel it again – the love-death beat
of his bodhrán: lub-dub, lub-dub, lub-dub –

as I lift bluebell seeds from a smudged
envelope. His scrawl requests that I share

only with those I love; they prefer, like him,
a damp climate, dappled light; they may

take years to flower. I see him now
as I scatter my packet over moist peaty soil,

see him harvesting in the constant wind,
off-white tufts of hair combed back

like cheviot fleece snagged on field wire.
I see him clutching a metal bucket to his chest,

bending ever-so-carefully to pluck tiny tepal-
chambers for their gems; their future blueprints.

THE GLASS HARVEST: LINDISFARNE

Wayside

Last night we spread the map
    on the kitchen floor, got the double-
    jointed history ruler to bridge
    the miles and miles between home
    and Holy Island.
Our son couldn't span the distance
    with his hand, so tried
    a foot instead, and tumbled:
    small highwayman flung
    from a dappled horse.
The whole journey long,
    his nose pressed against
    the glass, he asks:
    Are we there yet,
    the forest where Robin Hood hid?
Not yet son, soon. First
    the dereliction of the verges:
    shuttered pubs, neglected inns,
    unpatronised diners all falling into ruin –
    the great north road almost plundered.
By the time we arrive at the legendary hunting grounds,
    our freckled son is sleeping: tufts of hair
    sticking up from his green felt cap,
    its partridge feather bent, his toy bow
    dangling from the crook of his little finger.
The forest looms huge,
    tangled as any dreamscape,
    but he's in it too deep to wake,
    so we wait, and we wait,
    by the wayside.

Angel of the North

And when the child was a child,
kneeling in the footwell of a speeding
overheated car, her forehead
white against the blackened glass,
glancing in on other lives, other humans –
a vision made her head jolt back,

splay little bitten fingers and swipe
at the steamed-up triangle of window,
frantic to let her eyes revisit
the sudden gorgeous sighting of an angel,
sentinel on a hill. Rain-spattered,
double-exposed, superimposing itself

on her bones, her mind, her memory
some soothing blueprint for the future;
the image of its wide giant wings opened
in shelter (or the offer of an embrace
that had always been frustrated)
made everything slow to monochrome . . .

as though these first years of journeying
toward touch (fleet touch felt only
at the very edge of her senses)
would be stored somehow, able to sustain
her a long way beyond mother country.
Now technicolour; a prayer:

Dear angel, I have this ache in my chest
for a listener, a witness, someone I can whisper
to from inside my dark. Is it you who could hurt
when I do? You, who'd want nothing
but to shift down from your plinth
and buckle yourself all around me?

No Angel

What if we all have one,
an angel who leans
forehead to forehead
with us in libraries, on rooftops,
at the circus? What if
it is possible for another being
to know where it hurts
– just there –
without being told
where to stroke, press, probe?
I ache as I sit here writing
this, imagine you behind
or beside me, one hand
on my shoulder,
fingertips just brushing
my hair as though I matter . . .
I really matter. But no.
Even lovely bumbling Columbo
talks himself out
of what he senses close by.
There's that scene in *Wings
of Desire* where, leaning
against a snack van for a *cawfee*,
a *shmoike*, he mumbles,
(so close to his angel it is hell):
But you're not here, I'm here.
I wish you were here.
I wish you could talk to me.

Held

after 'Mary', 2016 by Miranda Boulton

It's the garden I want.
A quiet that isn't silence,
the garden holding onto its bowl-
ful of sun. I sit beside
the dried-up birdbath
nesting two egg-shaped pebbles,
sit listening to distant seals
lowing on the shore,
sit and listen to a titter
of birds quickening
as they perch to observe
me from a dusty wall, burst
into flight, as if frightened
by what they find: strange human
refusing to bloom.
Few flowers can thrive here,
but there's a snowfall
of blossom on the schoolyard
tree, a petalled horse
chestnut near the harbour
path and, close by, a host
of no-longer-lovely daffodils
wanes to an opaque, stained wax
paper that makes me feel
uncontained here –
constrained restrained detained
tear-stained – in pain here,
angel, come find me.

The Tidal Wife [01:24]

A fealty of water slapping
    rock-shore slows time
        here in mother country.

Weaving between prayers
    and footprints of other
        pilgrims, she's cut herself off

from the mainland to visit
    the unreachable places;
        to follow an urge to journey

into that gap between sad
    and unhappy. Living
        remotely like this for years

she seems muted to a vision
    of woman endured: all
        intimacy felt at a distance.

How to thrive in a silenced
    life? A silenced life minus
        the ongoing conversation

of bodies, minds, pasts;
    that unruly human cycle
        of pull and push; of solitude

then its opposite. She envies
        the intuition of the seas,
                how they know like a kind of

homing when to draw
        close, when to retreat.
                Something tries to rise in her

but cannot follow its course,
        at best she is blocked viaduct;
                conduit choked with weeds.

Pole to Pole

Chattering, we trek the silvered
poles onto a tiny tidal island.

You're nine: all gaps, blustered
plaits, a smirk as you relish

wet upsucks from glistering sand.
You'd wanted castles, magic,

a land so wild and wide it would
upend you from your wellies,

tip you howling back into the world.
We trudge at a slant for the listing,

wind-wracked church, grappling hands,
scarves horizontal, the crunch

of shucked glass and mussel shell
beneath our feet. Inside, the shock

of calm, all words measured, even
in rapturous song. You fiddle and split

a blonde crucifix, one eye blinkered
by the ancient heavy door rattling

in its frame, one ear tuned to the crash
and boom of the sea, restless in the dark.

I wonder if you would rather be out
in it too; if you carry the same unhinged

feeling where a storm is a sanctuary
and a church a kind of shipwreck.

Pearl

Imagine how it feels to grow
knowing you are nature's mistake:
a simple irritation,
a bit of grit that snags and chafes
within folds of soft wet flesh.

What if you were told
the rare event of you began
as a defensive measure?
A lustrous coat thrown over
some shameful naked object.

I see you in the bearded dark
of a barnacle-scarred shell,
set back in a clutch of muscle
hiding all your luminous beauty.
Come now, listen –

there is so little to cherish in display,
in opening, in trying to mime
pleasure (those all fall away).
What matters is what's left after
the root's been loosed,

a chin tipped up to sup
that strangely familiar taste:
sea – rust – love.
So much better the smile that spreads
and says you are the treasure, you.

Dollywash

Below the walled garden
of the seal-grey house,
between soft long grass
and gritty strands of sugar
kelp tangled where the tide left it:
five stone steps.
Follow them down to a well,

empty now but for rocks,
weeds, a knot of silver driftwood
and two crouching girls
cleaning fistfuls of dollywash
in the pit's dirty pool.
They rinse their smooth-edged
gems like washerwomen:

hems drenched, knees to ears,
swirling the circular eddies
between their legs.
They lift, spit, thumb-rub furiously,
then hold their treasures up
to the light, eyes wide, bright,
winking with pleasure.

*Dollywash – a Northumbrian word for seaglass

[65]

The Tidal Wife [07:15]

She bum-slides down a dune,
trips stupidly to the sea,
arms wide, eyes runneling.

A piece of driftwood stretches
out like a nude on satin sheets
and she knows she has to leave.

Growing up, she had no sense
of her body as her own:
private, mighty, beautiful –

her body never connected
to pleasure; its underground
longings sprung but ignored;

its usual movements muted,
all its callings falling silent.
Barefoot in the bleached weeds,

clusters of pale pink clam-
shells snap at her ankles
like barely hinged nails

and she thinks of her children,
and turns toward the water
tower near where her offspring

sleep. She shudders at a nothing,
or is it, perhaps, a something?
Guilt or shame for not wanting

to be the kind of woman
who shores all four corners
of her family without keeling –

but who wants nothing more
than to shimmy under a wire
fence to be totally, totally alone.

Boo to the Goosegirl

The island is retreating from the tide
and its designs on sinking the causeway.
Not halfway across, a goosegirl adrift
behind her flock: freckled feathers in her hair,
barefoot and songless, wilfully vacant
as though she's forgotten what was lost.

I want to shake her from her dream state;
wake her to her best parts exiled to silence,
compliance, self-denial; take her to task
for a lame faith she's best at tending small things –
(notice that gaggle of unruly thoughts
never yet stick-beaten into flight).

I want to face her like her own livid twin:
pinch her, punch her, scratch her and holler
about the dangers of her torpor. But then
I'll want to hold her, buoy her, reassure her
she'll be sea-changed for being woken
and hurried off this flooding causeway.

Causeway

No workmen or bulldozers
just two plucky women
ceaselessly trying to reach
one another despite winter
storms, rising tides, and
savage winds untamed from
Scandinavia. Daily they
strive – not so much to hold
back the tide – but to work
with it, around it, in
deference to its unstable
surge to spoil and spill and
gush across their toil; to
ransack any progress;
dismantle vague relations to
the mainland. Natural
drainage is compromised by
dams of sea-born debris:
silt, salt, wrack and
shattered shells all landed
at the tideline to amass
some fresh destruction.
And I know (god, how I
know) that it begins to feel
like a punishment: this
endless, joyless, repeating,
repeating, repeating, only
to witness the sea's deleting.

Kin

for Sarah Lambert

Orchid hunters, feverish
for a first sighting of *Epipactis Sancta*:
Lindisfarne's own rare breed.
I watch them from the dune slacks
of the snook on the island's western edge;
watch them from my hidey hole
in the marram where I lie low

(book spread-eagled on my chest)
thinking about my dead father's half-sister:
our long-lost family botanist.
I feel useless for not knowing
about plants or half-aunts:
how to find and identify them.
One day, after months of searching,

I'll track her down to a city garden
glasshouse and I'll begin to love her
as she teaches me how to differentiate
between Marsh, Tyne, Dune
and Lindisfarne – orchids all
the same to me: their yellow-green
leaves, teeth tiny at the margins,

their white-lipped petals like fists
clutching cupfuls of liquid.
They belong to the same family, she says,
but here is how you know a Sancta –
she lifts the flower's hood with her
little finger to reveal its brown interior.
Hazel, see? The same colour as our eyes.

Cloudberries

after Edwin Morgan

There were never cloudberries
like the ones we found
that tender afternoon
in peaty ruins
Lindisfarne Castle
a late autumn sunlight
wind moving in the dunes
heather staining the mainland
your pale hands emerging
from fingerless gloves
to uncover a little plant
preserved in salty darkness
you untucked its leaves
revealing three amber jewels
the first bruised to a juice
the second placed delicately
on your tongue your blue eyes
on mine my open mouth
watering to take the final honey
cluster between my lips
leaning side by side
our wellies kicked off
you urged me to abandon
my island living
walk the causeway beside you
my tight fist nestled in your palm

let me be beautiful
in that remembered light
precious as the rose gold lodes
coursing deep within
your highland hills
let me reach for you and follow

let the tide rinse away our tracks

The Tidal Wife [13:34]

Yesterday, the way he touched
    their son's hair, ever-so gently,
        whilst ushering him up for bed,

took his hand away, loss
    crossing his face, before
        he returned it, closed his eyes,

sighed. Or how their daughter
    likes to dangle from his neck,
        cling there grinning at him

and he seems surprised by it,
    surprised and delighted
        that she loves him with all

her uncomplicated heart.
    He locks himself away,
        keeps books face-down

on the nightstand, never takes
    his shoes off inside the home.
        Her only clue is that he persists

in placing his razor, toothbrush,
    and lense case among her eye
        cream, lip balm and tweezers –

despite having a shelf of his own.
  Stay, and a surface-smooth world
    won't need to change, they'll fill

out, go grey, soften in exhaustion,
  probably. Stay, and face another
    half a lifetime continuing to move

prudently around one another,
  enacting a far-off choreography
    that is the spit of perfect union.

A Pair of White Geese

In the silence
emptied of words,

a slight interruption
to the light, the flag-snap

of distant wings and a sound
like uncertain oboe notes

as a pair of white geese
fly over, conversing

in the thermals
of a laundered world.

I observe their superfluid
union, connected but

separate, necks extended
toward the sun

as they bank left, converge
with a chevron-shaped flock,

lift into the updrafts,
and vanish.

The Lone Migration of a Pink-Footed Goose

Dreading it all winter: spring,
        that instinct to return to an iced
                darkness I hardly dare recall
        yet sense exists somewhere,
elsewhere, inside of me or out,

pounding loud as any home-
        sickness yet subtle as the tap-tap
                inside a clutch of frail-shelled suns.
        My flock took wing without me
as I eyed them from the mudflats

picking at my patch of eel-grass,
        my angel wing good as useless,
                the other one beating for a homing
        and bewildered by the air's refusal.
Maybe, I thought, *I can settle for*

a migration of the mind, let flight
        follow the heart's intent. So, if I
                jut out my neck just like this –
        will some ghost of my shot body
still lift with my lost familiars?

* Angel Wing – a syndrome that affects aquatic birds causing the last joint
  of the wing to twist and stick out from the body.

Goose, Wounded

I want to tell you about the goose
wounded in the dune, one sore wingtip
scoring circles in the sand.
I want to describe the sight of his angel
wing: flight feathers stripped and twisted,
sticking out like sickly straws.
Each time I edge over, he ruffles
in distress, reminding me of the times
you try to reach for me and I fluster
at your touch, or those days I must escape
from you to curl into my private hurt.
But whose hurt should I attend to:
mine or the dying bird's? He moans
when I move too close, lumbers
backwards into a puddle of flood-water
that doesn't comfort, but when I go to leave,
hobbles lopsided until he plummets
into the lough, settling fractiously to roost
in the wrecked plumage of his entirely
flightless self. I nestle in the beachgrass
to watch over his final night, sink low
inside my featherdown coat –
nose over zip – wishing I could tell you
that I understand it now, how witnessing
him like this is a kind of visitation, or a gift.

The Tidal Wife [19:45]

A kittiwake's flight feather
sticks up from a stubbly rut.
She squats on the pathway,

plucks it up to stroke its silk
and stick it in her raggedy plait
as she dodges a fresh badger

scat beside a wad of dewed
fleece glistening like sea foam.
Later, the wreck of a gull,

the cage of it split, tassels
of plastic knitted in its ribs,
a shattered splinter of beak.

A sense of a self drawing
closer as she nears the cliffs,
her armpits slick, she picks

up a grey-veined pebble
rounded in the surf, sensing
that one day (but not today)

it will warm up to remind
her of a time she almost lost
all human touch. She sinks

her hands in the rich mud-
flats and with each release
of her fingers, the stink

of atrophy, of being here,
of being mortal and in decay;
all this bliss and muck and beauty

witnessed, but not yet shared;
everything mulching together
and she can at last be a part of it.

Night at the Broken Light Chapel

We spread our jackets at the foot of the broken
light chapel, sit eating, waiting for the basin of sun
to spill over now-flat waves. I note your bristles
becoming silver, think about telling you I like it
when you don't shave, choose not to watch you
readying the camera, its strap twisted at your neck,
nowhere close to noticing you've left the lens cap on.

This old sun is losing its lustre, but that long low
afterglow on your lobe, your throat, warms me
towards you. Remember that pre-children wedding
in Bilbao? A morning spent wilting at the Guggenheim –
everything white and curved and irregular.
Remember our slippery afternoon fuck left undone?
My petalled dress that wouldn't zip up, that death-
trap taxi up a mountainside at dusk, and a blaze of sun
sizzline like a fat pimento behind the half-dust church.

I remember all this as we tiptoe down this hill in utter
silence, both headlamps weak against the joyless dark,
the beams drifting to either edge of an untended
path – and I'm thinking: *this is mining country*; thinking:
coal under pressure is diamond; trying to think
of anything but the pit between our un-held hands.

The Glass Harvest

That night, I wandered out in my pyjamas
for a signal, stumbled to the path
and ran my fingers along its scorched flowers,
pausing woozily at this hot thought:
I don't know if my life is viable.

It was eye-contact, briefly, with a ewe,
a greyish ewe, in a blue-black field
that had me stop to pocket her wiry fleece,
not-quite-dodge dung in the shin-high thistles,
edge closer to the cliff and lie there belly-

down, my chin tilting over its ridge.
I groped in the dust for that same frayed rope
knotted to a rusty post, winched it around my fists
and, although it burned, lowered myself.
A salt wind buffeted my skin and scritched

at my still-sore throat. I coughed, lost footing,
jolted hard to the left and gashed my knee.
Even bleeding, I needed to see what the storm
had washed free: more crocks, jutting bones
a ripe crop of salt-scoured glass.

Lit

As for myself, I am splintered by great waves. I am coloured glass from a church window long since shattered. I find pieces of myself everywhere, and I cut myself handling them.

JEANETTE WINTERSON, *Lighthousekeeping*

It will be days before I'll know what to do
with it: this bagful of glass shivers, my bounty.

Here, see how this bottleneck slips
onto my finger? Or how this thick jar-end

gleams, now cleaned, after its emergence
in reverse from the crumbling cliff:

little breech from a dusty womb.
Sometimes I like to rub the smooth edges

on my wrists, feel the jigger of an old risk,
dulled now with time, hold onto a brokenness

that gave way to a whole. It hits like voltage
in the small hours – the still small hours

of our final night – (my first unfevered sleep):
I see a vase, so clearly it is crystal, coiled

inside, a string of tiny lights, all my harvested
glass packed in snug from base to cusp,

the switch flicked and a lamp lit
for my children; my children's children.

Acknowledgements

I would like to thank the editors of the following publications where some of these poems first appeared, or are due to appear: *Mslexia, Lighthouse, The Compass, Allographic, Stand, Numero Cinq Magazine, The Pickled Body, The Island Review, Mint: New Writing from ARU, The Emma Press Anthology of the Sea, Watermarks: Writing by Lido Lovers and Wild Swimmers & Three Drops from a Cauldron.* 'Touchstone' appeared on Rebecca Goss' website during Children's Heart Week, 2014. 'Winifred' was longlisted in the Rialto Nature Competition, 2015; 'Half-life of the Cockle' was shortlisted in the Frogmore Poetry Competition, 2016; an earlier version of 'Bone Houses' won 3rd prize in The Elmet Trust Poetry Prizes, 2016; 'Dollywash', 'The Glass Harvest' & 'Night at the Broken Light Chapel' were shortlisted for the Overton Poetry Prize, 2016; 'Before the Causeway' was longlisted in the Watermarks Poetry Competition, 2016; 'Nest, Eigg' was published on Angela Topping's Hygge blog, 2017.

Thanks to Lucy Conway, Eddie Scott and all at The Bothy Project for awarding my residency on Eigg in 2016. Grateful thanks to The Society of Authors who awarded me a grant to enable my travel. Many thanks also to Rody Gorman and David Eyre for the translation into Gaelic.

To Chris Hamilton-Emery, man of extraordinary bravery and patience, thank you! To Michael Bayley, Kate Swindlehurst, Esther Morgan, Fiona Benson, Rebecca Goss, Julia Copus, Jane Monson, Natalya Anderson, Sarah-Jane Roberts, Megan Hunter & Liz Dignam, thank you for your advice and guidance. Thank you to my poetry sisters in the Sidney Workshop: Lucy Hamilton, Lucy Sheerman, Clare Crossman & Joanne Limburg. But most of all to my near and far family, thank you for letting me retreat when I needed to.

This book has been typeset by
SALT PUBLISHING LIMITED
using Sabon, a font designed by Jan Tschichold
for the D. Stempel AG, Linotype and Monotype
Foundries. It is manufactured using Creamy 70gsm, a
Forest Stewardship Council™ certified paper from Stora
Enso's Anjala Mill in Finland. It was printed and bound
by Clays Limited in Bungay, Suffolk, Great Britain.

CROMER
GREAT BRITAIN
MMXVIII